NORTH MIDDLE SCHOOL LIBRARY

PUBLISHERS

Copyright © 2011 by Mitchell Lane Publishers. All rights reserved. No part of this book may be reproduced without written permission from the publisher. Printed and bound in the United States of America.

Printing   1   2   3   4   5   6   7   8   9

Blue Banner Biographies

Alicia Keys	Flo Rida	Megan Fox
Allen Iverson	Gwen Stefani	Miguel Tejada
Ashanti	Ice Cube	Nancy Pelosi
Ashlee Simpson	Ja Rule	Natasha Bedingfield
Ashton Kutcher	Jamie Foxx	Orianthi
Avril Lavigne	Jay-Z	Orlando Bloom
Beyoncé	Jennifer Lopez	P. Diddy
Blake Lively	Jessica Simpson	Peyton Manning
Bow Wow	J. K. Rowling	Pink
Brett Favre	Joe Flacco	Queen Latifah
Britney Spears	John Legend	Rihanna
Carrie Underwood	Justin Berfield	Robert Pattinson
Chris Brown	Justin Timberlake	Ron Howard
Chris Daughtry	Kanye West	Sean Kingston
Christina Aguilera	Kate Hudson	Selena
Ciara	Keith Urban	Shakira
Clay Aiken	Kelly Clarkson	Shia LaBeouf
Cole Hamels	Kenny Chesney	Shontelle Layne
Condoleezza Rice	Kristen Stewart	Soulja Boy Tell 'Em
Corbin Bleu	Lady Gaga	Stephenie Meyer
Daniel Radcliffe	Lance Armstrong	Taylor Swift
David Ortiz	Leona Lewis	T.I.
David Wright	Lil Wayne	Timbaland
Derek Jeter	Lindsay Lohan	Tim McGraw
Drew Brees	Mariah Carey	Toby Keith
Eminem	Mario	Usher
Eve	Mary J. Blige	Vanessa Anne Hudgens
Fergie	Mary-Kate and Ashley Olsen	Zac Efron

Library of Congress Cataloging-in-Publication Data
Krumenauer, Heidi.
  Flo Rida / by Heidi Krumenauer.
    p. cm. — (Blue banner biographies)
  Includes bibliographical references and index.
  ISBN 978-1-58415-906-3 (library bound)
 1. Flo Rida—Juvenile literature. 2. Rap musicians—United States—Biography—Juvenile literature. I. Title.
ML3930.F57K78 2011
782.421649092—dc22
[B]
                                                                                                2010014893

ABOUT THE AUTHOR: Heidi Krumenauer has written more than 1,100 newspaper and magazine articles. Since 2006, she's been a regular contributor to several print and online publications. Heidi's first book, *Why Does Grandma Have a Wibble?*, was released in 2007. She is also the author of *Brett Favre*, *Rihanna*, *Jimmie Johnson*, *Joe Flacco*, *Lady Gaga*, and *Sean Kingston* for Mitchell Lane Publishers. Heidi graduated from the University of Wisconsin–Platteville with a degree in Technical Communications Management. She is in upper management for a Fortune 400 insurance company. Heidi and her husband, Jeff, raise their two sons, Noah and Payton, in Southern Wisconsin.

PUBLISHER'S NOTE: The following story has been thoroughly researched, and to the best of our knowledge represents a true story. While every possible effort has been made to ensure accuracy, the publisher will not assume liability for damages caused by inaccuracies in the data and makes no warranty on the accuracy of the information contained herein. This story has not been authorized or endorsed by Flo Rida.

PLB

Blue Banner Biography

Chapter 1
Just Call Me 5

Chapter 2
Growin' Up Flo' 9

Chapter 3
The "Low" Down on the Top of the Charts 15

Chapter 4
Goin' With the Flo' 19

Chapter 5
True to His R.O.O.T.S. 23

Chronology 29

Discography 29

Further Reading 30

Works Consulted 30

On the Internet 31

Index 32

Flo steps out in New York City on March 19, 2010, with his cell phone in hand. After publicly giving out his personal phone number during a live television interview in April 2009, it is quite possible he's still returning all of his messages!

Just Call Me

Many artists say that their fans are important to them, but no one has taken that statement as far as rapper Flo Rida. In April 2009, Flo Rida gave out his personal cell phone number to the public during an interview with CNN's Shanon Cook.

"Three-oh-five, five-two-eight, two-seven-eight-six," he said, as he made the phone sign with his hand.

"Are you kidding? Is that seriously your cell phone number?" asked Cook. "You want thousands of millions of fans to call you?"

"Of course," he says. "If they can go out and buy my albums, I can at least make the sacrifice to holler at the few people who call. A lot of times I'm busy so they'll get my voice mail. And if I can speak to them and I have time, I always text back because I think that's very important."

He proved he wasn't joking when he showed his iPhone to the camera during the interview. And then he took a call. "Yo, this is your boy Flo Rida. What's your name? What's good?" Unfortunately, the caller must have been a little nervous and hung up without saying a word. Apparently,

Flo performs at the Y100 Jingle Ball in Florida on December 12, 2009. He admits he used to get nervous about getting on stage before large crowds, but he's done it so much that he enjoys it now.

that's not unusual. "Most of them hang up," he says. "They don't think it's really me."

Flo Rida says he receives a lot of phone calls, and while it's hard to respond to everyone, he answers about 30 percent of the calls and text messages. It seems he could be missing a lot of calls, though. When the MTV Newsroom attempted to call and leave him a funny message, they were told Flo Rida's voice mailbox was full.

Even months after first publicizing his cell number, Flo Rida was still encouraging his fans to give him a ring. On

December 12, at Y100's Jingle Ball 2009 at the Bank Atlantic Center in Miami, Flo Rida told the crowd to take out their cell phones and put them in the "a-yer." He gave out his number again, and his phone lit up immediately.

"I definitely feel blessed to have been making music for twelve years and still have a career that's so young," Flo Rida expressed on his website, OfficialFlo.com. "I don't take anything for granted because my fans could be spending their money on so many other things and instead they're buying my record. I look forward to giving them hot music, consistently." Apparently, publishing his cell number is one way that Flo Rida attempts to thank his fans in person.

Flo Rida's fans aren't only in the United States. He has become an international superstar, but he has worked hard to build up that fan base. "It's very important . . . the loyalty that they have overseas," he told Cook. "Sometimes they don't even know the language, and they can repeat a song."

Referring to having number one records in twelve different countries, he told Cook: "To me, that's like having nine lives. Most people don't even have an idea that you can really sell music overseas. I always love the fact that I can do things internationally. When I was going to school, I took the approach that I wanted to take international business versus just taking business classes. So I always had that approach prior to me doing music."

> "I don't take anything for granted. . . . I look forward to giving them hot music, consistently."

Flo was featured as one of the fittest guys in America in the June/July 2008 issue of Men's Fitness magazine. Being on stage has been one of his greatest workouts. "By the end of the night, I feel like I've done a trillion squats and situps," he says.

CHAPTER 2

Growin' Up Flo'

Tramar Dillard was born on December 16, 1979. He was the youngest child in a family of seven siblings—all girls. And one of them is his twin! "It was cool. It gives me a natural respect for women," he says.

Their father, a talented musician, left his family when Tramar was young. His mother raised their family in Carol City—one of the toughest neighborhoods in Florida. She provided a loving environment within their home. Outside on the street, it looked much different, with frequent shootings and widespread drug dealing.

"Growing up in the projects every day, you never know when you have to lay down on the ground because they're shooting or the police SWAT team is on the roof or something," he says in his biography on OfficialFlo.com. "My mother always instilled in us that you could be from the ghetto, but you don't have to be of it. Just about all of my friends have been to jail, but not me. Because when it came down to doing certain things, I decided to be a leader and do more positive things. I chose to stay on the right path regardless."

Music was what helped Tramar stay on that straight path. In an interview with Lisa Rinna and Joey Fatone on the Red Carpet of the 2009 Grammy Awards, he was asked what his musical inspiration was growing up. "I was always inspired by my household," he answered. "I love music. I'm definitely into it. My dad . . . he sang. He plays almost any instrument. My sisters . . . they sing music." And there were the more famous influences as well. Growing up, Tramar listened to all kinds of music by such artists as Marvin Gaye, Aretha Franklin, Otis Redding, Run DMC, LL Cool J, and 2 Live Crew. He also listened to his own sisters, who formed a local gospel group.

> "I was the only boy of seven siblings . . . growing up without my father. . . . I needed to make the most of my time on earth."

When Tramar was nineteen, his sister Julia died from complications due to bronchitis. She was only twenty-five. Her loss inspired him to use his own music to make a difference. "When my sister passed away, I woke up and realized what I had to do," says Tramar on his Billy Bush Artist Biography. "I was the only boy of seven siblings, all sisters, and growing up without my father. I realized that I needed to make the most of my time on earth. I want to utilize all of my God-given talents and give back in a way that others can benefit. My mother is so strong and I always admired her for her strength and showing me that by sacrifice and being level-headed, anything is possible."

Tramar was good at many sports and especially loved playing basketball, but he realized at a young age that music

On April 3, 2010, Flo went back to his Carol City neighborhood to host the First Annual Kids Spring and Break into Motivation event, part of his nonprofit organization Big Dreams for Kids. Local children enjoyed a mini ferris wheel, bounce houses, face painting, pony rides, and all the food they cared to enjoy.

would be a better career choice. He spent numerous hours making tapes in his grandmother's and aunt's garages. "I was just like, 'I'm further with this music and I'm going to give it my all.' No Plan B. With that being said, there've been a lot of ups and downs and everything, trials and tribulations, but everything that got in front of me, I surpassed it. So it just definitely motivated me to conquer a lot of things if I just had faith."

> "Without being grounded, you have nothing to stand on. Nothing lasts long if you don't start from the ground up."

In ninth grade, Flo Rida began rapping with a four-member rap group called the Groundhoggz, local favorites in the Miami area in the 1990s. Years later, he still considered himself part of the group. When asked about the meaning of the group's name, Flo Rida says in his biography on AtlanticStreet.com, "Without being grounded, you have nothing to stand on. Nothing lasts long if you don't start from the ground up."

According to the school, Tramar graduated from Carol City Senior High School in 2000. He then studied international business management at the University of Nevada, Las Vegas, for two years, and at Barry University in Miami for two months. He dropped out before graduating to pursue a music career.

His first big break came at age eighteen through his brother-in-law, who was the hype man for Luke (Luther Campbell) of 2 Live Crew—responsible for backup rapping, singing, and getting the audience excited during concerts. Flo Rida was given the chance to do the same thing for Fresh Kid Ice, also of 2 Live Crew. In 2001, he started touring with this nationally recognized group. It wasn't long before he had gained the attention of DeVante Swing, formerly of the famed R&B group Jodeci. "After I got off tour [with Fresh Kid Ice], I got the chance to pass my demo to DeVante," Flo Rida says in his biography. "He heard it and wanted to fly me out to Los Angeles that day. I ended up flying out the next day, and stayed in L.A. for three years."

During that time, he worked with Swing and tried to land a record deal, but instead he remained broke, lived on the streets, and worked numerous odd jobs just to make a few bucks. He once had his bag confiscated by the Los Angeles Police Department. He'd left it on a bench at the Beverly Center mall, and police thought it might contain a bomb. False alarm!

"There'd been a lot of crazy things going on before I had success," he told *USA Today* in 2008. "I've had jobs paying $3 an hour—like digging through trash trying to find silverware when I worked at a casino in Las Vegas. I had to sacrifice because I needed studio time. It hasn't been a piece of cake or an easy walk. I was literally on the streets, at times promoting myself by myself," he says. "I always had the drive to push my own music. People tend to help you more when they see that you promote yourself. They know you're serious then."

> "I had jobs paying $3 an hour— like digging through trash trying to find silverware . . . I had to sacrifice . . ."

There's nothin' "Poe" about Flo Rida now that he's become an international rap star. This big piece of bling highlights the name of Flo Rida's record company, Poe Boy Entertainment.

The "Low" Down on the Top of the Charts

In 2006, Flo Rida was still determined to make it in L.A. He was trying to get his big break when he got a call from Poe Boy Entertainment's CEO, Elric "E-Class" Prince. Flo Rida's reputation for the work he'd done with DJ Khaled and the mix tapes with his high school friend, Rick Ross, were finally reaching the top. "E-Class told me that different A&Rs were hearing my music and they wanted to put my face on it," he says. An A&R—or artist and repertoire executive—is responsible for finding and developing new talent.

Flo Rida returned to Miami, where he signed a deal with Poe Boy Entertainment and then with Atlantic Records a few months later. "That was the greatest moment of my life," he recalls. "I had been working so hard for so long. I had jobs in construction, I worked in warehouses, I'm talking about some of the bummiest jobs. But those were all the sacrifices I made by putting my money towards my music, and it finally paid off."

Over the next year, Flo Rida worked on his debut album, *Mail on Sunday*, which was released on March 18, 2008. He didn't do it alone, though. He enlisted the help of

Flo performed "Low" with T-Pain during the 2008 BET Awards at the Shrine Auditorium in Los Angeles. He was nominated in two categories: Best New Artist and Best Collaboration ("Low" with T-Pain), but he didn't win either award.

several hit makers for production and vocals, including will.i.am, J.R. Rotem, Sean Kingston, T-Pain, Lil Wayne, Brisco, Rick Ross, Trey Songz, Yung Joc, Birdman, and Timbaland. While some of the songs on the album are "party songs"—designed for the clubs—there are others that bring out Flo Rida's personal side. "All My Life" is a song about losing his sister. "Me & U" is about staying together.

While many of the *Mail On Sunday* songs were successful, none hit the charts as hard and as fast as "Low," which was released several months before the album. It debuted—on November 6, 2007—at number 91 on the U.S. Billboard Hot 100 and reached number 1 by December 30. Featuring T-Pain, "Low" gained international popularity and was featured on the sound track album to the Disney film *Step Up 2: The Streets*, which was released on February 14, 2008. In 2009, "Low" garnered two Grammy nominations for Best Rap/Sung Collaboration and Best Rap Song. While he didn't win, it was a great honor to be nominated.

> "I didn't know 'Low' would get this big. It's the greatest feeling in the world."

Of his collaboration with T-Pain, Flo Rida told Jane Stevenson of *Sun Media* in June 2008, "Both of us being from Florida, it really did get us together to collaborate. But, definitely, the chemistry was there. I got into the studio and this was as fast as I'd recorded a record. It was, like, an hour. It was, like, verse after verse. There was a lot of my homeboys in there, different girls, and we had champagne. I think that's what really came across on the record. I didn't know 'Low' would get this big. It's the greatest feeling in the world."

Atlantic vice president of marketing James Lopez agreed. "This may seem like an overnight sensation to most of the country. The song spread so much faster than we could travel." The company's director of digital marketing, Brian Dackowski, said, "This phenomenon was organic. We haven't had an artist take off like this before with a song

Flo didn't get his start on **American Idol**, *but his popularity allowed him to perform on the same stage.*

picking up and kids across the country going for it on their own. It was like riding a wave."

With the success of *Mail on Sunday*, Flo Rida was in demand. He made guest appearances on other R&B, rap, and pop singles, including "Move Shake Drop" by DJ Laz, "We Break the Dawn" by Michelle Willams, the remix of "4 Minutes" by Madonna, "Running Back" by Australian R&B singer Jessica Mauboy, "Feel It" by DJ Felli Fel, and the remix of "Speedin" by Rick Ross. He also appeared on FOX's *So You Think You Can Dance* and *American Idol*, but he wasn't a contestant—he was already living the life of a superstar.

Goin' With the Flo'

Only a year after "Low" dominated the charts, Flo Rida was back again with "Right Round," the first single off his second album, *R.O.O.T.S.*, released on March 31, 2009. In its debut week, according to Billboard.com, the song was downloaded 636,000 times. That shattered the previous record, which was also set by Flo Rida—"Low" was purchased 467,000 times in its debut week.

"Right Round" was a fresh sound for an old favorite by Dead or Alive that had launched to the top of the charts in 1985. Their song "You Spin Me Right Round (Like a Record)" became popular again in 1998 when it was featured in the movie *The Wedding Singer*. Again in 2009, "Right Round" had a huge following, but this time Flo Rida's name was on the label. And this time, "Right Round" became the fastest-selling digital single in history, with over 2.2 million sold in just six weeks.

According to Flo Rida, the song is about "a young lady, . . . she's got my head spinning round . . . or any young lady that I might see walking past me that's getting my attention. She got it going on! I'm going crazy over her."

"Right Round," no doubt, played a role in the popularity and success of *R.O.O.T.S.*, which was nominated for a 2010 Grammy for Best Rap Album. Each year brings out the best of the best, but on January 13, 2010, Grammy blogger Dantrel Robinson, wrote: "This year's Grammy nominees embody the spirit of rap music's versatility. No matter who wins, 2009 is when rap galvanized its place in music history with a powerful blend of longevity, innovation and passion that transcends gender, race, socioeconomic status, and geography."

> "Initially when I first started out, it was very scary to get out on stage, but now I do it so much I enjoy it."

Flo Rida found himself in the hunt for the coveted golden gramaphone with rappers who were a bit more seasoned: Eminem, Mos Def, Common, and Q-Tip. Even though Eminem won the Grammy, it was an honor just to be nominated for such a prestigious award and to be included in an impressive group of nominees.

For a guy with a complex schedule and fast-paced record sales, it may seem that Flo Rida's life and personality are also complex. Not true. In fact, he told interviewer Shanon Cook, "Most people see me on stage and they think that I'm this crazy dude, but for the most part I'm a little shy and laid back." With all of his success, it would probably be easy for Flo Rida to become too confident in his music and his stage performances. "I love performing," he told Kim Halling of *The Voice Tv* during an interview in Sweden in 2008. "Initially when I first started out, it was very scary to

Flo attended the 2009 premiere of Walt Disney's G-Force. Flo and Nelly Furtado recorded "Jump," the movie's theme song.

At the 51st Grammy Awards in February 2009, Flo was nominated for Best Rap/Sung Collaboration ("Low" with T-Pain) and Best Rap Song ("Low" with T-Pain), but he didn't bring home any awards.

get out on stage, but now I do it so much I enjoy it. It's a way to vent out and not be so shy. A lot of times after the show, I'm like, wow, I did that?"

Flo Rida's music is important to him, and he wants to know that his fans get the most from the music he makes and performs. "I look forward to people just falling in love with Flo Rida. I love music. I want people to get the chance to feel my vibe."

CHAPTER 5

True to His R.O.O.T.S.

When Tramar Dillard changed his name to Flo Rida, he had a plan. He wanted something that would represent who he really was and what he wanted to portray to his audience. He's been asked many times what his name means and he always responds with: "Flo represents the melodic style I have. The Rida represents my gift to speed up or slow down my lyrics." While his stage name may have changed before he found fame, he admits his mother still calls him Tramar. "When she's playin' around, she'll say, 'Hey, Flo Rida.'"

Not only does his name reflect who he is and what he stands for, so do the tattoos on his arms and back. Flo Rida proudly sports a tattoo of Jimi Hendrix on his left arm. After being introduced to Hendrix's music by a family member, Flo Rida bought himself a DVD of Hendrix on tour. "Just to see an African-American rocker of his level was just amazing to me," he told Cheryl Thompson of *CHARTAttack* in May 2008. "You know he played the guitar left-handed, and from my point of view, he was a very laid-back dude until he got on stage and he was very electrifying and that kind of reminded me of myself. I'm also laid-back, but people are

Across Flo's entire back is a tattoo of a beach in Florida. Flo isn't shy about telling people how much his home state means to him.

amazed when I get on stage by some of the things I may say or do. I was like, if I was going to get a tattoo—which was my first tattoo—I wanted to get something that was different than anyone and that was out of the norm, so that's why I got Jimi Hendrix."

As part of a 2009 concert series for NBC's *Today* show, Flo entertained a crowd at Rockefeller Center in New York City.

During the 2009 MySpace Music Awards, Flo had to get a little "Low" to speak to one of his shorter fans.

Sprawled across his entire back is a tattoo of his home state—Florida—representing his loyalty to the state where he grew up. "Yeah, I call it a mural because it has the lifestyle of South Beach, and then to the 'hood where I grew up in Carol City, 37th Ave. projects . . . ," he told Thompson. "It's the place I was born. I can't forget about Florida. It means the world to me. I've been everywhere . . . love it, but there's no place like home. Especially growing up in Miami. You've got the hot beaches and the different cultures—Dominican, Puerto Rican, Cuban, Haitian, Jamaican. And there's all different types of food I can enjoy."

Flo Rida's roots and heritage have always been important to him, so it is no wonder that he titled his second album *R.O.O.T.S.*, an acronym for "Route of Overcoming the Struggle." The inspiration for the title came from his trip to Africa in 2008. "I had a chance to go to Africa for the first time for the MTV Africa Music Awards," he says in his biography. "It was spiritual. It was amazing to see so many black people. I felt goose bumps . . . the fact that I'm doing something I love and it took me to this point of visiting the Mother Land. It was an amazing experience."

During that time in Africa, Flo Rida became more aware of the struggles that Africans face, and it made him think about the personal struggles he faced while growing up in the projects in Florida. "I was definitely inspired by the fact that I had a chance to go to Africa . . . but going back to my neighborhood, you know, I had a lot of struggling too, where it was a lot of drug dealing around me. My mother always taught me and my sisters that if you can believe it, you can achieve it. This album gives my fans a chance to know me as a person, prior to my success. And right now I'm happy that the world looks at me as a great leader as far as me doing my music and coming with a positive approach."

Flo Rida has become a leader in more than just his music. On December 7, 2009, he teamed up with the Grammy Foundation and performed at a fund-raiser in Pittsburgh, Pennsylvania, to support breast cancer awareness. Flo Rida

> "My mother always taught me and my sisters that if you can believe it, you can achieve it."

and Grammy-nominated British act The Ting Tings performed at the Soldiers and Sailors Memorial Hall, with all proceeds going to the Glimmer of Hope Foundation.

From the gang-infested streets of a tough neighborhood in Miami to the Red Carpet of the Grammy Awards in Los Angeles, Flo Rida is pursuing the dream that was born within him as a young man. "It's amazing," he said in an interview on *Hiphop.com*. "A lot of the time I do feel like I'm dreaming. I can recall not having a song or enough money to go to the studio. This is while I'm watching people win Grammys and People's Choice Awards. I say to all aspiring artists: I came from nothing, and if I can do it, anyone can do it."

> "I say to all aspiring artists: I came from nothing, and if I can do it, anyone can do it."

CHRONOLOGY

1979*   Tramar Dillard is born on December 16
2000*   Graduates from Carol City Senior High School
2001   Goes on tour with 2 Live Crew
2006   Signs with Poe Boy Entertainment and Atlantic Records
2007   His first single, "Low," is released on November 6
2008   Releases debut album, *Mail on Sunday*, on March 18; travels to Africa for the MTV Music Awards; is named one of the Top 25 Fittest Guys in America in the June/July 2008 issue of *Men's Fitness* magazine
2009   Releases his second album, *R.O.O.T.S.*, on March 31; wins a People's Choice Award for Favorite Hip Hop Song—"Low" featuring T-Pain
2010   Attends the 2010 Grammy Awards; is nominated for Best Rap Album; hosts the first event for his new charity, Big Dreams for Kids

* Sources vary regarding Flo Rida's birth date and graduation date. Some sources say he was born on September 17 and that he graduated in 2001.

DISCOGRAPHY

Albums
2009   *R.O.O.T.S.*
2008   *Mail on Sunday*

Singles
2009   "Right Round"
        "Sugar"
2008   "Elevator"
        "In the Ayer"
        "Jump"
        "Be on You"
2007   "Low"

Books
While there are no other young adult books about Flo Rida, you may enjoy these other Blue Banner Biographies from Mitchell Lane Publishers:

Bankston, John. *Eminem*. Hockessin, DE: Mitchell Lane Publishers, 2004.

O'Neal, Claire. *T.I.* Hockessin, DE: Mitchell Lane Publishers, 2010.

Torres, John A. *Lil Wayne*. Hockessin, DE: Mitchell Lane Publishers, 2010.

Wells, PeggySue. *Fergie*. Hockessin, DE: Mitchell Lane Publishers, 2008.

Works Consulted
51st Annual Grammy Awards (2009): "Lisa Rinna & Joey Fatone Interview Flo Rida at the 2009 Grammy Awards!" http://www.fancast.com/tv/The-51st-Annual-Grammy-Awards/103316/1036066532/Grammys-2009-Flo-Rida/videos

B96 Chicago: Radio 96.3 FM http://www.b96.com

Billy Bush Artist Bio: "Flo Rida" http://www.billybushshow.com/playlist?action=viewArtist&artistID=98

Cook, Shanon. "Flo Rida Answers the Call." *CNN.com*, April 8, 2009. http://www.cnn.com/2009/SHOWBIZ/Music/04/08/flo.rida/index.html

Crosley, Hilary. "Rapper Flo Rida Puts on 'Sunday' Best." *Reuters.com*, January 19, 2008. http://www.reuters.com/article/idUSN1934639920080122

Flo Rida's Page: Atlantic Street http://www.atlanticstreet.com/profile/FloRida

Flo Rida "The TODAY Show" Video. July 24, 2009. http://hiphop.popcrunch.com/flo-rida-the-today-show-video-07-24-09/

Halling, Kim. "Flo Rida Interview." *The Voice Tv*, July 23, 2008. http://www.youtube.com/watch?v=f6UyTQIuhlk

FURTHER READING

Jones, Steve. "On the Verge: The Sunshine State of Flo Rida." *USA Today*, March 14, 2008.
http://www.usatoday.com/life/music/news/2008-03-13-flo-rida_N.htm

"Meet the 2008 MF 25." *Men's Fitness*, June/July 2008.
http://www.mensfitness.com/fitness/287

Pietroluongo, Silvio. "Flo Rida Topples Single-Week Download Mark." *Billboard.com*, February 18, 2009.
http://www.billboard.com/news/flo-rida-topples-single-week-download-mark-1003942356.story

"Rida on the Storm." *Hiphop.com*, March 27, 2009.
http://metarefreshcode.com/ftest/52-flo-rida-interview

Robinson, Dantrel. "It's a Rap! — A Look at Rap in 2009." *Grammy.com*, January 13, 2010
http://www.grammy.com/blogs/its-a-rap-%E2%80%94-a-look-at-rap-in-2009

Stevenson, Jane. "Flo Rida Riding High with 'Low.'" *Canoe.ca*, June 27, 2008.
http://jam.canoe.ca/Music/Artists/F/FloRida/2008/06/27/6007791-sun.html

Thompson, Cheryl. "Flo Rida: Bigging Up Miami Hip-Hop." *CHARTattack.com*, May 30, 2008.
http://www.chartattack.com/features/53030/flo-rida-bigging-up-miami-hip-hop

On the Internet

Atlantic Records: Flo Rida
http://www.atlanticrecords.com/florida

Big Dreams for Kids
http://www.bigdreamsforkids.com

Flo Rida's Official Web Site
http://www.officialflo.com

PHOTO CREDITS: Cover, pp. 1, 22 — AP Photo/Chris Pizzello; pp. 6, 8 — Ray Tamarra/Getty Images; p. 6 — John Parra/WireImage/Getty Images; p. 11 — Vallery Jean/Getty Images; p. 14 — Ian Gavan/Getty Images; p. 16 — Frank Micelotta/Getty Images for BET; p. 18 — Frank Micelotta/American Idol 2009/Getty Images for BET; p. 21 — Eric Charbonneau/Le Studio/Getty Images; p. 24 — Raymond Boyd/Michael Ochs Archives/Getty Images; p. 25 — Theo Wargo/WireImage/Getty Images; p. 26 — David Livingston/Getty Images. Every effort has been made to locate all copyright holders of material used in this book. If any errors or omissions have occurred, corrections will be made in future editions of this book.

INDEX

2 Live Crew 10, 12
American Idol 18
Atlantic Records 15, 17
BET Awards 16
Cook, Shanon 5, 7, 20
Dackowski, Brian 17
Dillard, Julia (sister) 10, 16
Eminem 20
fans 4, 5–7, 22
Fatone, Joey 10
Flo Rida (Tramar Dillard)
   in Africa 27
   awards and honors for 17, 24
   birth of 9
   collaborations of 16–17, 18, 20, 28
   and charity work 11, 27–28
   childhood of 9–12, 26
   education of 12
   family of 9, 10, 27
   on Florida 24, 26
   heritage 9, 26, 27
   hobbies of 11
   influences on 10
   jobs of 13, 15
   name change for 23
   on shyness 20, 22
   tattoos of 23, 24, 26
Fresh Kid Ice 12–13
Furtado, Nelly 21

G-Force 21
Grammy Awards 10, 17, 20, 22, 28
Groundhoggz 12
Hendrix, Jimi 23, 24
Jodeci 12–13
Kids' Spring and Break into Motivation 11
Lopez, James 17
"Low" 16–17, 19
Mail on Sunday 15, 16, 18
Men's Fitness 8
MTV Africa Music Awards 21
NBC's *Today* show 25
Poe Boy Entertainment 14, 15
Prince, Elric "E-Class" 15
"Right Round" 18, 19, 20
Rinna, Lisa 10
Robinson, Dantrel 20
R.O.O.T.S. 19, 20, 27
Ross, Rick 15, 16, 18
So You Think You Can Dance 18
Step Up 2: The Streets 17
Swing, DeVante 12–13
Ting Tings, The 28
T-Pain 16, 17, 22
University of Miami 12
University of Nevada, Las Vegas 12
Y100 Jingle Ball 6, 7